Opposites

playBac PUBLISHING
More.Brain.Power

Big or small, short or tall, discover the wonderful world of opposites!

Full of dynamic photographs that demonstrate the amazing diversity of our world, EYE LIKE OPPOSITES is a perfect tool to help your curious child learn this fun concept. Each eye-catching spread explores the uniqueness of being unalike with opposites that exist in nature.

So what are you waiting for?
Whether you go fast or slow, there is plenty left to know! Let's go!

3

Big

elephant

Small

ladybug

Big and small,
the elephant tall
towers over the others with a nod,
"True friends are just like peas in a pod."

peas

mouse

ants

zebra

Front

Back

rabbit

"Hello."
"Goodbye."
"My, oh, my," the rabbit sighs,
"where do you start and where do you end?"
"I'll tell you," the zebra replies,
"if you can figure out why my stripes
bend!"
Back and forth the two
friends go, until there is
nothing left to know!

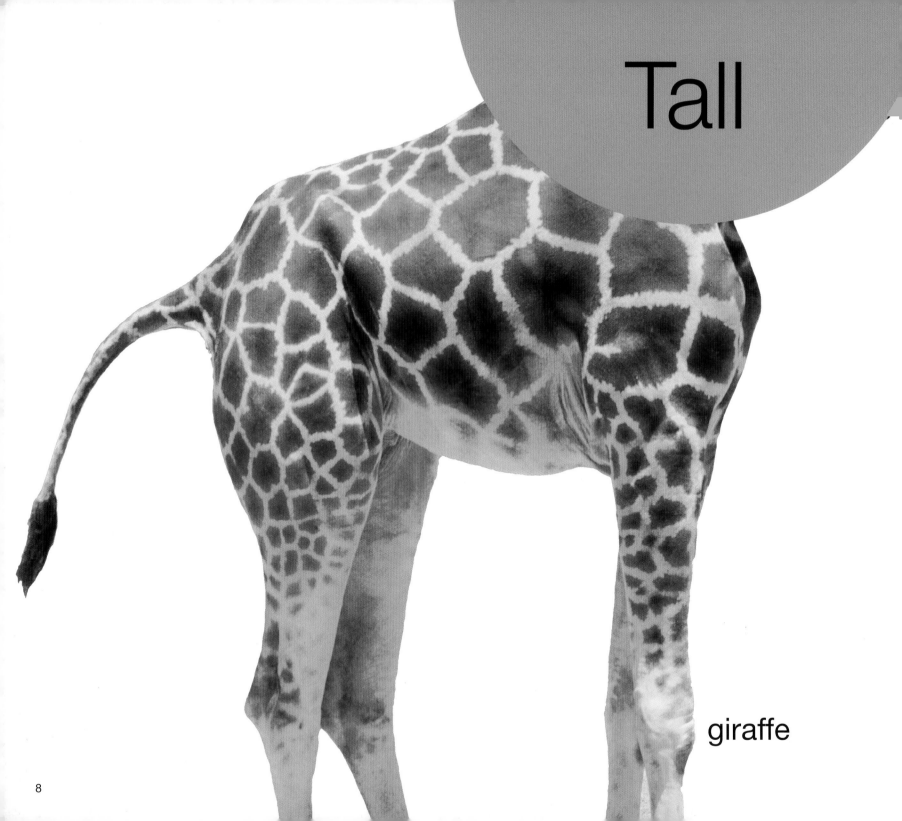

Tall

giraffe

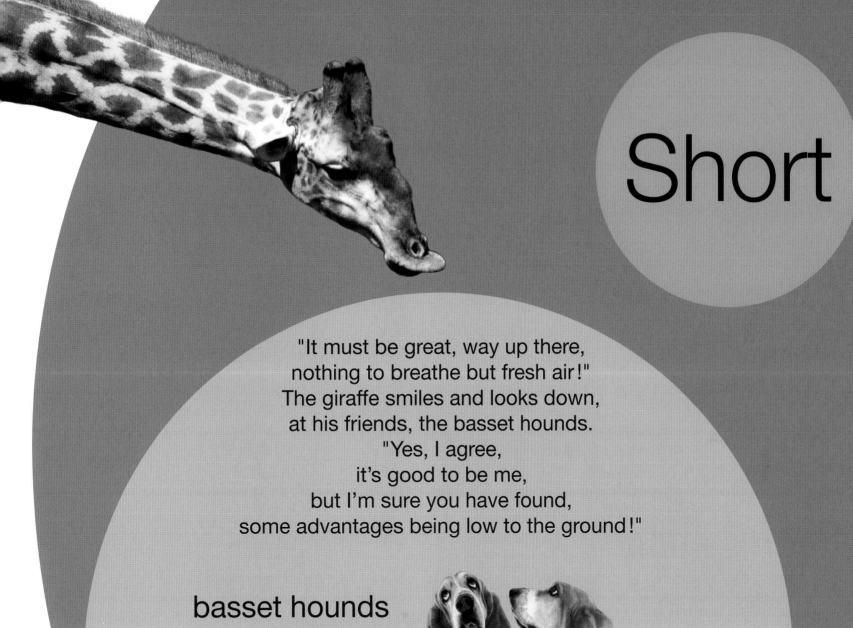

"It must be great, way up there,
nothing to breathe but fresh air!"
The giraffe smiles and looks down,
at his friends, the basset hounds.
"Yes, I agree,
it's good to be me,
but I'm sure you have found,
some advantages being low to the ground!"

basset hounds

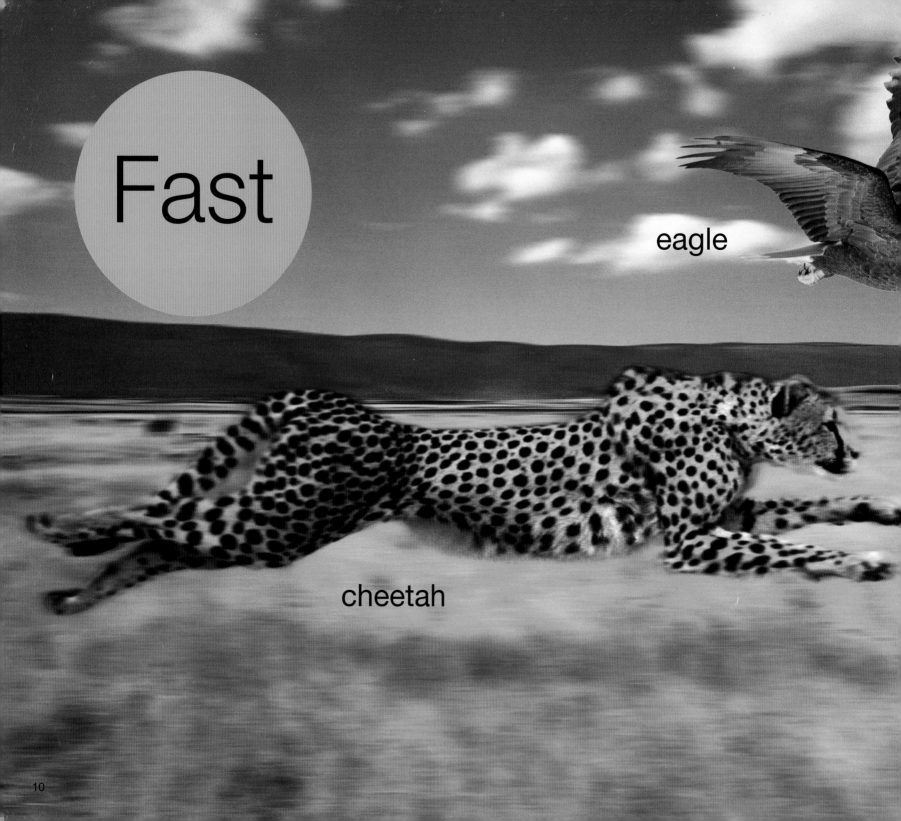

Fast

eagle

cheetah

Slow

"Let's go!"
"Let's race!"
"Only if we can set a slower pace."
The turtle and snail are tired of these games;
they always seem to end the same!

turtle

snail

Young

sapling

hatchling tortoises

When I was a hatchling,
I was really something!
I remember a day
when I could quickly run away.
I, too, remember when I was young and fre
and not yet a full-grown tree!

olive tree

giant tortoise

Old

Black

blackbird

black bear

blackberries

White

goose

"My feathers are dark, and yours are light,"
the blackbird says with a bit of delight.
The goose replies with a bit of a sigh,
"I work day and night
to keep them so bright."

lily

polar bear

15

Above

crane

clouds

"I wonder what it would be like to fly so high.
Perhaps I should give it a try."
And so the mongoose tries with all his might,
but no matter what, he just can't take flight.
"Oh well." He looks to the sky.
"I guess I'll just watch the crane pass by."

16

mongoose in its burrow

Below

Top

reindeer's horns

pineapple

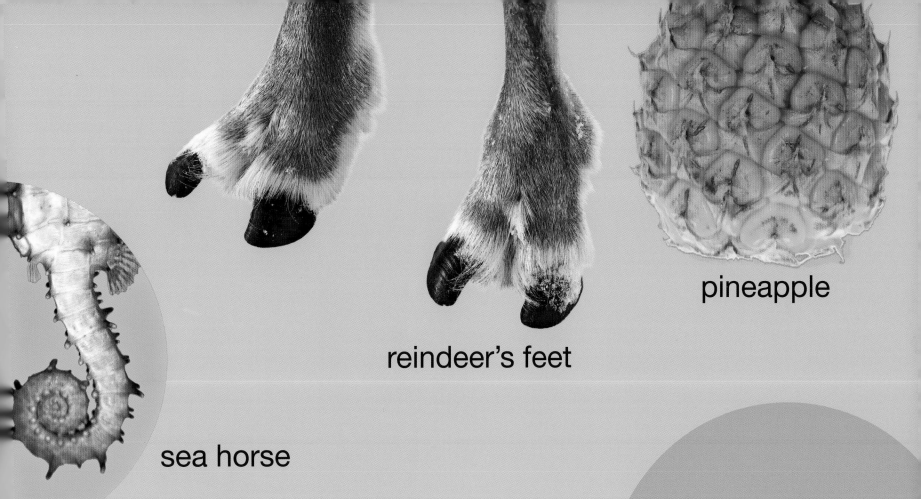

pineapple

reindeer's feet

sea horse

For every bottom,
there is a top.
The question is:
Where does one begin,
and the other stop?
The reindeer and the sea horse ask each other.
The pineapple would never bother.

Bottom

19

Rough

stormy sea

If you look closely
at the stormy sea,
there are many things
for you to see:
The wave crashing down,
and water swirling all around.
Now take a look
at the peaceful lake,
and the tiny ripples
the water makes.
Both the lake and sea
are made of water,
but their personalities
couldn't be odder!

lake

Smooth

Many

How many flamingos do you see?
Let's count, 1… 2… 3…
Oh boy, there are just too many,
let's just say their numbers are plenty.
On the next page
– give it some thought –
how many flamingos
can you spot?

flamingos

None

woodpecker in its nest

In

My home is my shell,
it is here that I dwell –
when I'm "in."
"I make my home in trees.
I come and go as I please,"
says the woodpecker,
out on a limb.

snail in its shell

Out

woodpecker flying

snail out of its shell

Asleep

bear cub

"Come on, come on, let's play!"
"I'm ready to go, let's get underway!"
The lemur and penguin can't wait
to go and have fun,
but the puppies and cub are already done –
sound asleep and dreaming deep.

puppies

penguin

Awake

lemur

bat

moon

owl

The bat and owl stay up late,
all night long they like to debate!
When the sun rises
they have a few surprises:
They've reached a stalemate
and need to recuperate!

Night

Day

sun behind poppies

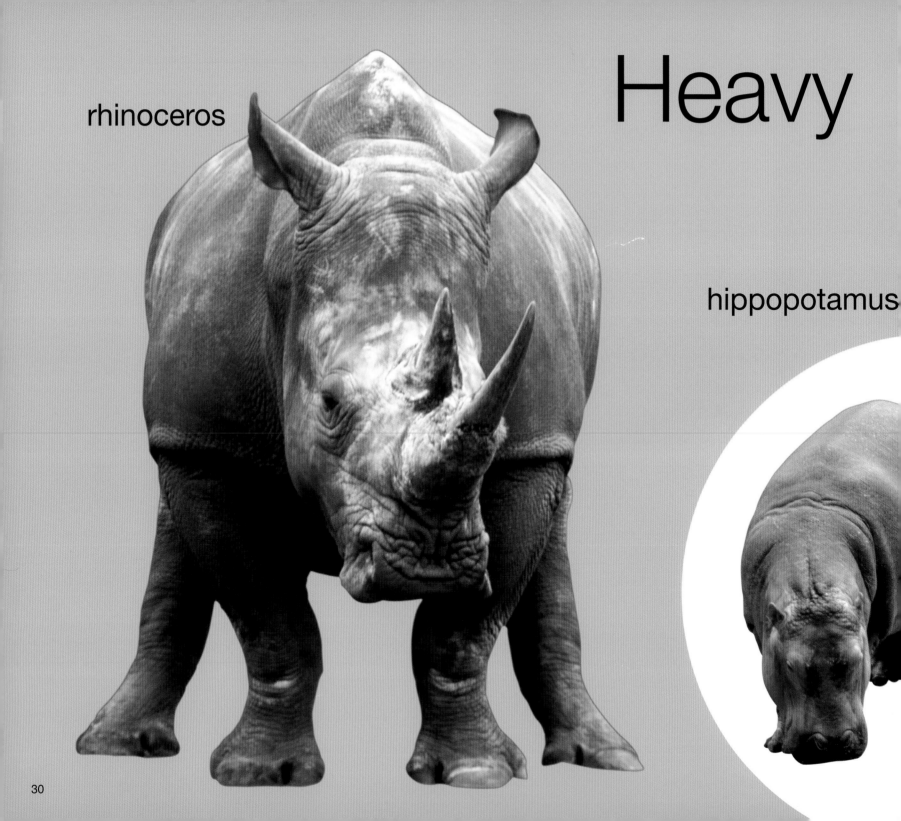

rhinoceros

Heavy

hippopotamus

Light

feather

petals

"I weigh more than you!"
"I don't believe it, that can't be true!"
The hippo and rhino want to see
just how heavy they might be!
The butterfly
doesn't even try!
"I'm light and I'm limber
so that I can fly!"

butterfly

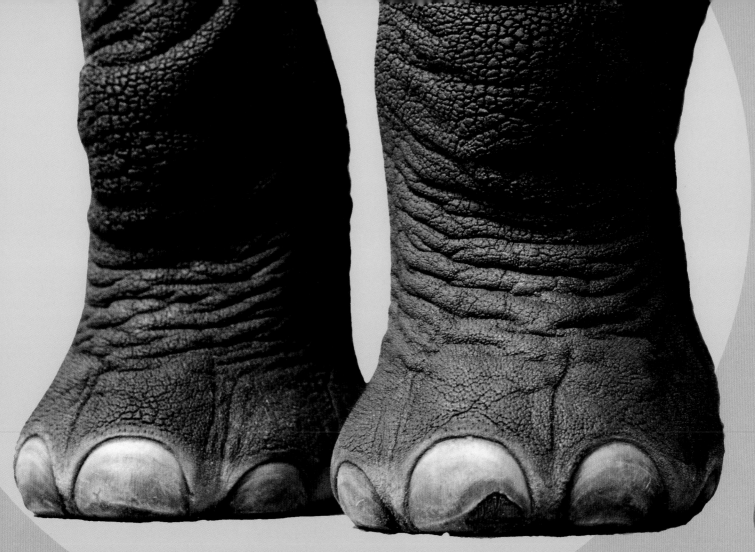

elephant's legs

mushroom

Thick

Thin

asparagus

stick insect

Through thick or thin
I see an elephant shin!
Thin or thick?
Here's a bug built like a stick!

Closed

Sometimes things don't look like much,
some boring pods and shells and such.
But beauty sometimes hides inside,
waiting, waiting to open wide.
Then what perfection you will see,
a walnut and a red poppy.

poppy

walnut

Open

walnut

poppy

Near

impala

Look at me
I'm right here.
Way up front, very near.
But look beyond my handsome face,
to find the wildebeests giving chase!

Far

herd of wildebeest

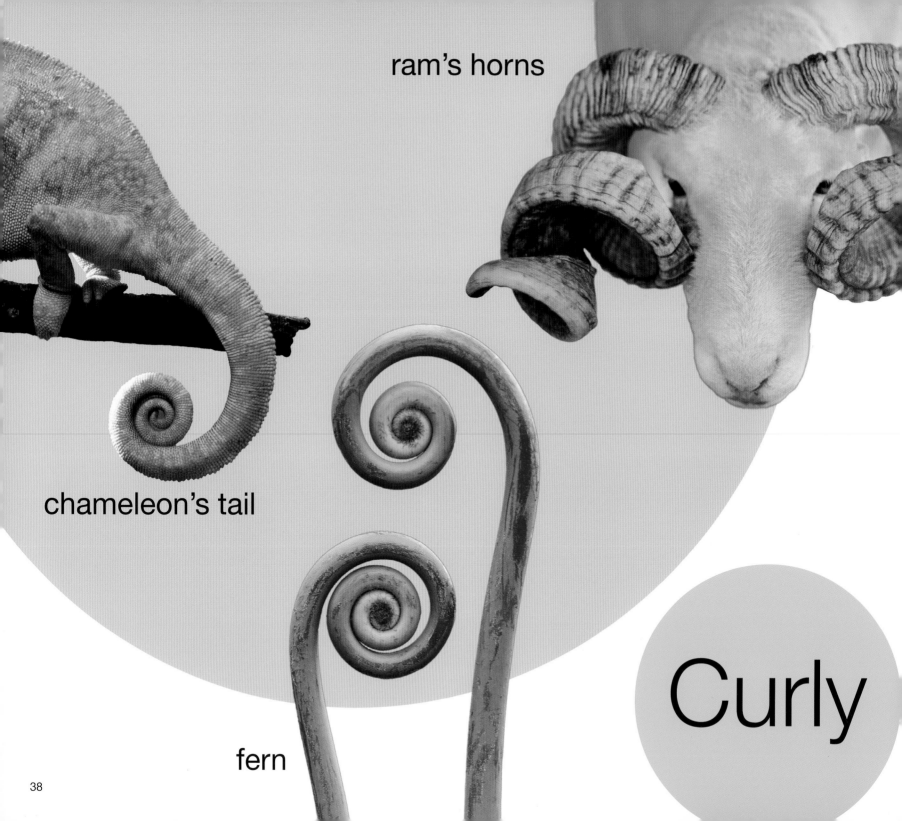

ram's horns

chameleon's tail

fern

Curly

Straight

dog's tail

The fern likes to furl
and the chameleon's tail does a swirl.
Curly or straight?
No need to debate –
the lines of nature always fascinate!

bamboo

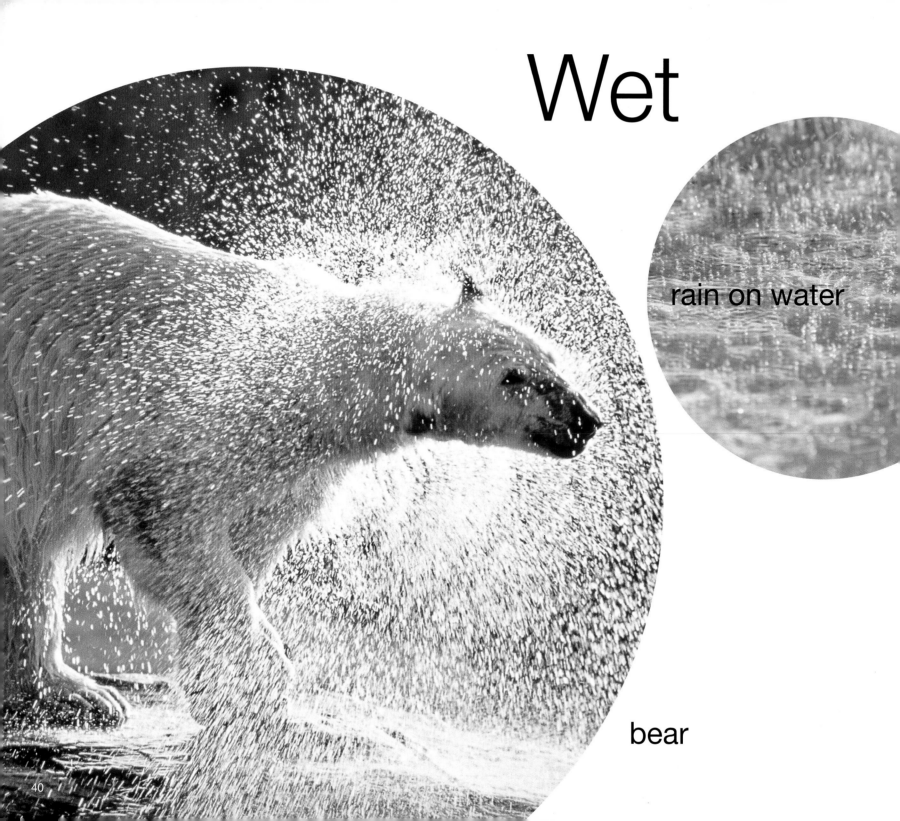

Wet

rain on water

bear

"Oh, this water feels nice,
especially after living on ice!"
Water is very important, the polar bear knows,
without it, nothing grows!

Dry

desert

leaf

"Boo hoo, look at you.
You both appear sad through and through."
The dolphin isn't trying to be mean,
he's just stating what he's seen.
To help his friends feel better again,
he mentions that laughter's the best medicine!

bull dog

Sad

rabbit

dolphin

Happy

chimpanzee

43

Bald

egg

vulture

Hairy

This vulture isn't so sure
if baldness has a cure.
"Don't worry," says the caterpillar.
"Hair is merely filler."
"That's right," agrees the ram.
"Hair is just a small part
of who I am!"
"With or without,
you're great – no doubt!"

caterpillar

ram

Noisy

zebra

magpie

Quiet

Haw!
Caw!
Well, that's the last straw!
There's no need to tease.
We may need to call in the referees.

monkey

fish

Just a part is not a whole.
One slice, one petal, is not our goal.
When they meet, they are complete.
The flower, the orange, cannot be beat!

daisy petals

orange segments

Part

Whole

orange

daisy

Brave

Unlike the ostrich with its head
in the sand, these jungle dwellers
will take a stand.
They make a fierce pair.
"Come near, if you dare.
We have no fear, so beware!"

chimpanzee

leopard

ostrich

Cowardly

Tame

border collie

kitten

The lion lets out a mighty roar.
In the wild he likes to explore.
The tame, small kitten can only say:
"I hope I can roar like you one day!"

Wild

lion

horse

Hot

volcano

Red sparks fly
through the dark night's sky,
as the volcano erupts
and lava bubbles up.
"It may look warm and bright,"
the penguin does appreciate
the light.
"But I feel much safer,
over here on my ice wafer!"

Cold

iceberg

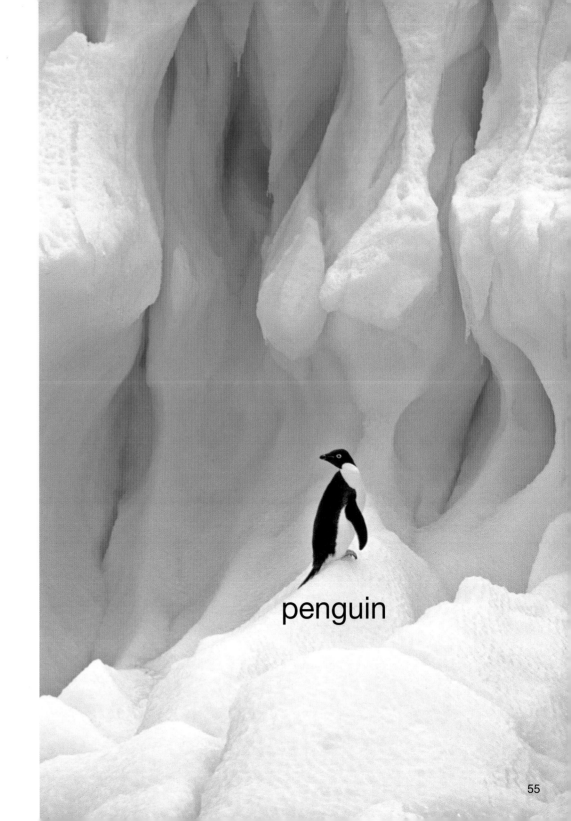

penguin

Acknowledgments:

Play Bac Publishing wishes to thank all the teachers, mothers, and children who have helped develop the **eye like** series.

SPECIAL THANKS to: Alain Pichlak, Frederic Micaud, Ingrid Biraud, Véronique Malite, Gregory Rutty, Anne Burrus, and Paula Manzanero.

Copyright © 2008
by Play Bac Publishing
USA, Inc.

ISBN-13: 978-1-60214-054-7

Play Bac Publishing USA, Inc.
225 Varick Street, New York, NY 10014-4381

Printed in Singapore by TWP

Distributed by
Black Dog & Leventhal Publishers, Inc.
151 West 19th Street, New York, NY 10011

Photography credits:

Meaning of the letters:
h : top ; b : bottom ; d : right ; g : left ; c : center.

BIOS: Alcalay Jean-Jacques 1&9h ; Klein J.-L& Hubert M.-L 6d&back cover ; Klein J.-L& Hubert M.-L 7g&back cover ; Klein J.-L& Hubert M.-L 26b ; Klein J.-L& Hubert M.-L 53d ; Krasemann S.-J / Peter Arnold 10h ; Gilson François 11 ; Gilson François 33d ; Thiriet Claudius 25d ; Lattes Emmanuel 24 D ; Labat Jean-Michel 32d.

CORBIS: DLILLC -1&47d ; Christopher Talbot Frank/Solus-Veer 29 ; Envision 31d ; Envision 34g ; Frans Lanting 0&38c ; Jose Fuste Raga 38d ; Craig Tuttle 40g ; Steve Lupton 48g.

CORBIS / ZEFA: Herbert Kehrer 40d ; Adrianna Williams 39d.

EYEDEA / HOA-QUI: Mark Jones/Age 13g&57 ; Age 18b-19h ; Mark Hamblin/Age 19h ; Philippe Bourseiller 54 ; Montheath ED. House 55.

EYEDEA / JACANA: Sylvain Cordier 16h ; Tom Walker 18g ; Jouan/Ruis 27d ; Laurent Tangre front cover&spine&34d.

EYEDEA / JACANA /NPL: Paul Hobson -1&46d ; George Mc Carthy 28g ; Ingo Arndt 45b.

GETTY: Gavin Hellier front cover ; Dorling Kindersley front cover&spine&34d ; America Images Inc. 1&52d ; Hiroyuki 2d&42d ; Bob Elsdale 2g&50g ; Klaus Nigge 3d&24g&spine ; Gail Shumway 3g&25g ; panoramic Images 6g&46d ; Catherine Ledner 6g ; Ryan Mc Vay 7d ; Guy Crittenden 8 ; Gandee Vasan 9b ; Frank Lane/Parfitt 10 ; GK Hart / Vikki Hart 11D ; Jeff Foott 12c&56g ; David doubilet 12h&56h ; Rosemary Calvert 12b ; Michael Melford 13d ; Richard H Johnston 20 ; Eastcott Momatluk 21 ; Michael Poliza 22 ; Michael Durham 28h ; David W. Hamilton 26h ; Darrell Gulin 26g ; Claudia Uribe frontcover&31g ; Franck Greenaway 31c ; Jim Naughten 31h&58 ; James Hager 36 ; Richard Dutoit 36-37 ; Tim Flach 38g ; Sakistyle 39 ; Gregor Schuster 41d ; Jim Reed 41 ; Terry Husebye 42g ; Howard Berman 43d ; Peter Anderson 45d ; Micheal Simpson 47c ; Michael Rosenfeld 48c ; James Balog 50d ; Steve Bloom 51 ; Steve Shott 52d ; Dorling Kindersley 53d.

PHOTONONSTOP: Mauritius 18-19 ; Westmorland 43g.

SUNSET: Lacz Gerard : 16-17 ; Juniors Bildarchiv : 44d.

OTHER PHOTOS: DR.

In the same series: